I0807513

INSIDE MLS

CF MONTREAL

BY BRIAN TRUSDELL

SportsZone

An Imprint of Abdo Publishing
abdobooks.com

abdobooks.com

Published by Abdo Publishing, a division of ABDO, PO Box 398166, Minneapolis, Minnesota 55439.

Printed in the United States of America, North Mankato, Minnesota
052021
092021

THIS BOOK CONTAINS RECYCLED MATERIALS

Cover Photo: David Kirouac/Cal Sport Media/Zuma Wire/AP Images
Interior Photos: Paul Chiasson/The Canadian Press/AP Images, 5, 6, 8–9; Ryan Remiorz/The Canadian Press/AP Images, 10, 13, 41; Denis Brodeur/NHLI/National Hockey League/Getty Images, 15; Ray Stubblebine/AP Images, 16; Andre Pichette/AP Images, 19; Graham Hughes/The Canadian Press/AP Images, 20, 23, 24, 33, 39; Aaron Doster/AP Images, 26; David Kirouac/Icon Sportswire/AP Images, 29; Aaron Doster/Cal Sport Media/AP Images, 30; Peter McCabe/The Canadian Press/AP Images, 34; J. P. Moczulski/The Canadian Press/AP Images, 37; Chris Young/The Canadian Press/AP Images, 42

Editor: Patrick Donnelly
Series Designer: Dan Peluso

Library of Congress Control Number: 2020948217

Publisher's Cataloging-in-Publication Data

Names: Trusdell, Brian, author.
Title: CF Montreal/ by Brian Trusdell
Description: Minneapolis, Minnesota : Abdo Publishing, 2022 | Series: Inside MLS | Includes online resources and index.
Identifiers: ISBN 9781532194764 (lib. bdg.) | ISBN 9781098214425 (ebook)
Subjects: LCSH: National Professional Soccer League--Juvenile literature. | Soccer--Juvenile literature. | Soccer teams--Juvenile literature. | Professional sports franchises--Juvenile literature. | Sports Teams--Juvenile literature.
Classification: DDC 796.334--dc23

TABLE OF CONTENTS

CHAPTER 1

MAKING AN IMPACT

The situation looked bleak for the Montreal Impact. It was March 3, 2015. The Major League Soccer (MLS) club was facing Mexican team Pachuca. It was the second leg of their Concacaf Champions League quarterfinal. A week earlier, the teams had tied 2–2 in Mexico.

That alone was quite an accomplishment for the Impact, who are now called Club de Foot (CF) Montreal. Canadian and US clubs have not fared well in the tournament against their more established competition from across the region. Only two MLS teams had ever won a Champions League game in Mexico. Only four others had managed a draw in 26 tries. And only one MLS team had ever beaten a Mexican team in a knockout series in the Champions League.

Montreal's Ignacio Piatti, right, *and Pachuca's Jorge Hernandez race to the ball.*

telcel
SAMSUNG
CEMENTOS FORTALEZA
adidas
BMO

Bakary Soumaré (5) and Calum Mallace celebrate the Impact's late comeback against Pachuca.

A first-leg draw on the road was a promising result for the Impact.

However, in Montreal for the rematch, Pachuca's Germán Cano converted a penalty kick in the 80th minute. That lead stood as the game entered stoppage time. The 38,104 fans in Montreal's Olympic Stadium were desperate for a goal. At any moment, the referee might blow his whistle to end the game. But then Montreal midfielder Calum Mallace took possession in his team's defensive end.

He saw 21-year-old Cameron Porter streaking down the left side of the field. Mallace lobbed a long ball over the defense. Porter managed to stay onside and settled the ball off his chest at a full sprint just outside the penalty area. He brushed off a defender and shot the ball between the legs of the Pachuca goalkeeper.

Olympic Stadium erupted. Porter was buried under his ecstatic teammates. The Impact had tied the score. When the referee ended the game moments later, the crowd set off smoke bombs. Blue and white flags waved. The noise inside the stadium was deafening.

It was only a 1–1 draw. But that was good enough for Montreal to advance. The teams had tied 3–3 on aggregate, or total goals in their two games. However, the tiebreaker fell in Montreal's favor. The Impact had scored twice in their game in Mexico, and Pachuca had only scored once in Canada. Montreal was the winner on away goals.

ON TO THE FINAL FOUR

The victory sent the Impact to the semifinals of the tournament, which featured the top clubs in North America, Central America, and the Caribbean. Montreal was only the

Impact goalkeeper Evan Bush makes a diving save in the first match against Alajuelense.

fifth MLS team to get that far. Not bad for a club with the worst record in MLS a year earlier.

In 2014 the Impact won only six of 34 games. They were outscored 58–38. So Montreal was certainly not considered one of the top MLS teams. Yet here it was in 2015, two steps from going to the Club World Cup.

Two weeks later, the Impact hosted Alajuelense of Costa Rica in the first leg of the semifinals. Once again the game was at Olympic Stadium, which held more fans than the Impact's usual home field nearby. The crowd of 33,675 was in for a treat. Ignacio Piatti and Victor Cabrera scored first-half goals and Montreal won comfortably 2–0.

Impact fans came out in full force to cheer their team on to victory.

Three weeks later, the teams met in Costa Rica for the second leg. It was the beginning of April, and while the weather was still chilly in Canada, it was hot and humid in Costa Rica. But the weather didn't affect the Impact early. Jack McInerny managed to score a goal three minutes before halftime to put the Impact ahead 1–0. Up 3–0 on aggregate, surely Montreal could feel safe.

However, the Impact's advantage took a major hit early in the second half. Pablo Gabas scored twice in a 13-minute span to rally Alajuelense to a 2–1 lead. Montreal fans began to have flashbacks to 2009, when it had blown a similar lead in a Champions League series against a team from Mexico.

Instead, the Impact responded as Andres Romero scored in the 72nd minute to tie the game 2–2. Montreal had restored its two-goal aggregate lead with 18 minutes to go.

But the drama was far from over. Allen Guevara put Alajuelense back in front 3–2 in the 79th minute. Montreal still led 4–3 on aggregate. Even if Alajuelense scored another goal to tie the aggregate, Montreal had already scored twice in Costa Rica and would win again on away goals.

Alajuelense did score again in stoppage time. But Montreal was able to run out the clock. Alajuelense won the match 4–2 to tie the aggregate score, but the away goals tiebreaker sent the Impact through to the finals. They were only the second team from MLS and the first team from Canada ever to reach the finals.

The Impact's magical run continued against Club América, one of Mexico's most popular teams. The teams drew 1–1 in Mexico in the first leg. All Montreal had to do was win at home and the Champions League title was theirs.

A crowd of 61,004 showed up at Olympic Stadium. They exploded as Romero gave the home team a lead with an early goal. But in the second half, Montreal allowed four goals in 31 minutes and lost 4–2. Still, it was an impressive run for the Impact to show they were the second-best team in Concacaf.

"It's been a whole team effort," Montreal coach Frank Klopas said. "Regardless of the outcome tonight, I'm extremely, extremely proud of what our team has accomplished."

BEST SEASON

The Champions League run kept the Impact occupied until late April 2015. Meanwhile, the MLS season started on March 7. The overlap didn't go well for Montreal. It remained winless in league play until May 16. But then the turnaround began. The Impact won four of their next five games. They went on to finish with the seventh-best record in the league. Through 2020 it remained the best finish in team history.

Club president Joey Saputo, *right*, comforts defender Laurent Ciman after the Impact lost to Club América in the final match.

CHAPTER 2

LE FOOTBALL DE QUEBEC

The original rules of association football—also known as *soccer*—were written 1863 in London, England. From there, the game quickly spread to Britain's former colonies, which included Canada.

In 1911 the Province of Quebec Football Association was formed in Montreal, Canada's second-largest city. Montreal is the largest city in the Canadian province of Quebec. Many people there speak French as their first language.

As immigrants arrived in Canada, they brought aspects of their culture with them. A love of soccer was one of them. Immigrants formed soccer clubs that helped develop the game in Canada. Businesses also sponsored teams. Some of the earliest teams were Grand Trunk, Montreal Carsteel,

Hockey legend Gordie Howe plays soccer with Montreal youth in the early 1960s.

EATONS
LAVAL

Dwight Lodeweges (5) of the Montreal Manic fights off Steve Moyers of the New York Cosmos in a 1983 NASL match.

and clubs for players from Czechoslovakia, Hungary, Ukraine, and Italy.

Some Canadian soccer leagues were considered professional. However, the talent level and interest in the game didn't compare to the leagues in Europe and South America.

By the 1960s, a few professional leagues had come and gone in North America. Finally, a league with some staying power was formed. The North American Soccer League (NASL) started in 1968. The first Montreal team to enter the league was Olympique in 1971. Montreal had recently been awarded the 1976 Olympic Games. The team took its name from the well-known world sports festival.

Olympique was not very good. The team never won more than five games in a season and folded after three years. Graeme Souness of Scotland was one of its top players. As an 18-year-old he was named to the NASL First All-Star Team. Another notable player for Olympique was forward Jim Corsi. He went on to become a goalie in the National Hockey League (NHL).

LE MANIC

Le Manic's name came from the Manicouagan River in northeast Quebec, where a large hydroelectric dam was a source of pride for Quebec residents. Other names also in contention included Chinook, Kayak, and Borèal.

Professional soccer didn't return to Montreal until 1981. The Philadelphia Fury were looking for a new home, and they relocated to Quebec. The team was renamed the Montreal Manic, or just *Le Manic* in French.

The Manic fared better than Olympique. They made the NASL playoffs in each of their three seasons. They drew 58,542 people to a playoff game in 1981. And in 1983 the Manic shocked the NASL by defeating the mighty New York Cosmos in the first round of the playoffs. However, the team folded in 1983, and a year later the NASL did too.

Montreal's next pro team, the Supra, formed in 1988. It played in the Canadian Soccer League. When that league folded in 1992, Supra ownership decided against joining the American Professional Soccer League (APSL). Instead, they sold to food services businessman Joey Saputo. Many of the Supra's players and coaches joined Saputo in the minor league APSL to form the Impact.

MINOR LEAGUE SUCCESS

The Impact did well for an expansion team, winning the league playoff title in their second season. The league went through a number of name changes, including stints as the A-League and the United Soccer Leagues (USL) First Division. But the Impact's success was one constant. They finished the regular season with the league's best record in 1995, 1996, and 1997. League playoff titles followed in 2004 and 2009.

Impact goalie Greg Sutton, *left*, celebrates with Gabriel Gervais and Adam Braz after beating the Seattle Sounders 2–0 to clinch the 2004 A-League championship.

Also in 2002, supporters of the Canadian national team came up with a trophy called the Voyageurs Cup. It was given to the team who had the best record among Canada's USL teams. Montreal won it the first six years. In 2008 the cup was awarded to the winner of a separate tournament among the top teams in Canada. Again, Montreal won it.

Eventually Impact management turned its eye to MLS. Toronto had been awarded a team in 2005 and began play in

Captain Mauro Biello raises the trophy as the Impact celebrate winning the 2009 USL First Division championship.

2007. The league announced in July 2008 that it wanted to add two teams for the 2011 season. Montreal was a candidate.

But later that year, Vancouver and Portland were chosen instead. In 2009 Saputo and MLS commissioner Don Garber resumed talks to bring MLS to Montreal. A year after that, Montreal was officially granted an MLS team.

TAKING THE NEXT STEP

It took another two years, but the Impact played their first game in MLS in 2012. Their 2–0 loss to the Vancouver Whitecaps was a bit of an omen. The Impact finished their first season with the 12th-best record out of 19 teams.

But in 2013, they posted a winning record, qualified for the playoffs, and won the first of two straight Canadian Championships. In 2015 the Impact had their best season in MLS, finishing third in the Eastern Conference. They also beat archrival Toronto Football Club (FC) in the playoffs and reached the finals of the Concacaf Champions League.

The Impact saw many famous players come through their locker room. Ivorian forward Didier Drogba arrived in 2015. He had made his name with Chelsea in the English Premier League. Others included Italian defender Alessandro Nesta, Ignacio Piatti of Argentina, and Italy's Marco Di Vaio, who became one of the team's all-time leading scorers. However, by 2021 the club hadn't achieved what it hoped, on or off the field. It decided to make a fresh start and change its identity, which included a new name: Club de Foot Montreal.

"To make an impact," Saputo said, "we need to retire the Impact."

2013 PLAYOFFS

Montreal reached the MLS Cup playoffs in only its second season in the league. It was quite an accomplishment, but it did so only barely. The Impact won their first four games of the season. But they won only one of their last eight games. Montreal clinched the final playoff berth in the Eastern Conference in the last week of the season. Despite a 1–0 loss to Toronto, it qualified for the playoffs when Chicago also lost.

CHAPTER 3

INTERNATIONAL INFLUENCE

Montreal is a cosmopolitan city, so it makes sense that the Impact's first MLS star would come from Europe. Italian striker Marco Di Vaio was the team's first Designated Player. That means he was signed to a contract outside the league's limits on salary. He had played for some of the biggest clubs in Europe, including Juventus and Lazio in Italy and Monaco in the French league. He also played for the Italian national team.

Di Vaio didn't join the Impact until midway through their first season and scored only five times. But in his second year, he scored 20 goals. That was the third-most in MLS and only two behind the league leader.

Marco Di Vaio, right, *wrapped up a long, successful career with three seasons in Montreal.*

adidas
BMO

Didier Drogba quickly made a difference when he joined the Impact in 2015.

Unlike many of the other star players in MLS at the time, Di Vaio wasn't flashy. Instead, he was known for precision with his chances and getting into good position to score. His best game came on May 25, 2013. Di Vaio scored three goals in the first 32 minutes in a 5–3 victory over the Union.

Di Vaio was nearing the end of his career when he joined Montreal. He came to the Impact just before his 36th birthday.

He played three years before retiring from soccer in 2014. His 34 career goals rank him among the best in team history.

PREMIER LEAGUE LEGEND

Several big-name players have suited up for Montreal. None, however, came to the club with more advance headlines than Didier Drogba. The forward from Ivory Coast signed with Montreal on July 27, 2015. That was just two months after he won his fourth English Premier League title with Chelsea. Drogba's 104 career goals placed him fourth all-time in Chelsea's long history. He also had played in three World Cups and scored 65 goals in 105 international appearances.

Montreal proved to be a good fit for the French-speaking Drogba. He made his debut as a sub against Philadelphia on August 22. Then in his first start two weeks later against the Chicago Fire, he scored three goals to lead Montreal to a 4–3 win. Drogba scored 11 goals in 11 games, his last two coming a minute apart against Toronto FC in the final game of the season. First he redirected the ball with the inside of his left heel into the net. Then he deflected the ball in with the outside of his right foot to rally Montreal to a 2–1 victory. The Impact lost just twice in their final 11 games and finished with the best record in their history.

Evan Bush has more appearances for Montreal than any other goalkeeper in club history.

Drogba's second season with Montreal wasn't as successful. He played twice as many games but scored just 10 goals. He was 38, which is old for soccer players, particularly forwards.

EVAN BUSH

One of Montreal's most unsung heroes was an American goalkeeper. Evan Bush was with the Impact when they joined MLS. He didn't become the regular starter until the 2015 season, but he became a fixture in goal until being traded during the 2020 season. His stellar play in 2015 earned him the Concacaf Champions League's Golden Glove Award as the tournament's top goalkeeper.

He had knee and back problems, and the club held him out of games on artificial turf to protect his body. Drogba helped Montreal reach the Eastern Conference finals in the playoffs but left the team after the 2016 season.

A STAR FROM ARGENTINA

Ignacio Piatti came to the Impact with much less hype than Drogba or Di Vaio. He was younger, hadn't played with many big teams, and he'd never played for his national team in Argentina. But in the end, Piatti played in more games for Montreal than the other two combined. He also scored more goals and is considered by many to be Montreal's greatest player.

Piatti had played most of his career in his native Argentina. But he also played with smaller teams in the French and Italian leagues. In 2015 he scored nine goals, two fewer than Drogba, and was named the team's most valuable player. He won that honor again in 2016, 2017, and 2018. He led the team in scoring in each of those years.

Piatti was selected to three MLS All-Star Games and twice was named to the MLS Best XI. He was known as a technically gifted player, a midfielder able to dribble around a slew of defenders in tight space and thread a ball behind opposing defenses. After the 2019 season he returned to Argentina, but not before becoming Montreal's career leader with 66 goals and 35 assists.

JOEY SAPUTO

Although not a player or coach, Joey Saputo may be the most important person in team history. With the backing of his family's dairy company, Saputo started the Impact in 1992. He guided the team through its early days and then sold it to a group of investors in 1999. But when the team went bankrupt in 2001, Saputo rescued it. He led the push to make the Impact an MLS team, which finally happened in 2010.

HOMETOWN HERO

Patrice Bernier was born in the Montreal suburb of Brossard, Quebec. He began his professional career with the Impact as a 20-year-old when it was competing in the lower divisions of North American soccer. He left to play in Norway, Germany, and Denmark

Ignacio Piatti (10) and defender Tommy Smith of the Colorado Rapids fight for the ball in a 2018 match.

Midfielder Patrice Bernier was a steadying force for the Impact's first six MLS seasons.

before returning to help the Impact launch its first season in MLS in 2012.

A familiar presence in midfield, Bernier—a regular on the Canadian national team for more than a decade—became the team's second captain. He retired in 2017 near the top of the team's career leaders with 151 games played, 15 goals, and 25 assists.

HERE COMES HENRY

One of the highest-profile signings in Montreal history was not for a player. Prior to the 2020 season, the team hired Thierry Henry to become its seventh head coach since joining MLS. Henry had been one of the world's most prolific scorers during his playing days, especially with English club Arsenal. He had also helped France win the 1998 World Cup. Like Drogba, Henry was attracted to Montreal's French heritage.

Henry had a tough task rebuilding a team without Piatti. His first season also came during the COVID-19 pandemic, forcing Montreal to play home games in New Jersey. Despite this, Henry showed promise in his first season in charge. He proved he could adapt to different challenges and helped the team's young players improve. And, despite some rough patches, Henry guided Montreal back to the playoffs for the first time since 2016.

CHAPTER 4

CANADIAN CLASSIQUE

The contrasts between Montreal and Toronto are clear, especially on the soccer field. In Montreal most people speak French, and they cheer for a team in blue uniforms. In Toronto most people speak English and root for a team that wears red.

CF Montreal was born as a minor league club in 1992. Toronto FC took the field 15 years later, bypassing the minor leagues for MLS. Still, a longstanding rivalry between Canada's two biggest cities has led to mutual disdain between the two teams and their fans.

Known by some as the Canadian Classique, the rivalry between CF Montreal and Toronto FC is also called the 401 Derby. The name comes from the road that stretches

The action is always intense when Montreal and Toronto meet on the soccer field.

BMO
BMO

Montreal's Pato Aguilera tracks Jim Brennan (11) of Toronto FC during the clubs' first Canadian Championship match in 2008.

roughly 330 miles (530 km) between Montreal and Toronto. It's called Highway 401 on the Ontario side of the border.

Whether in ice hockey, football, or even baseball, Montreal and Toronto have been competing in sports for more than a century. The rivalry between the NHL's Montreal Canadiens and Toronto Maple Leafs began in 1917. It's one of the most storied in all of sports. However, through 2020 the Canadiens and Maple Leafs had gone 40 years without facing each other in the playoffs. Some fans argue the intercity rivalry now is carried by CF Montreal and Toronto FC.

KINGS OF CANADA

The conflict between the teams began in 2008, four years before the Impact joined MLS. They met in the Canadian Championship, a tournament between the country's top professional teams. In 2008 that tournament included Toronto and minor league teams from Montreal and Vancouver.

The first time they played each other, Toronto won 1–0 in Montreal on a 72nd-minute goal by Marco Vélez. But each team had to play the other teams twice, once at home and once away. The team finishing with the best overall record won the title.

Montreal defeated Vancouver twice, both times 2–0, while Toronto lost at home 1–0 to the Whitecaps and drew 2–2 in Vancouver.

That set up a final pivotal game in Toronto for the title. All Montreal needed was a draw and it would finish atop the three-team standings. In front of a red-clad sellout crowd of more than 20,000 at BMO Field in Toronto, the home team took an early lead. But Montreal's Roberto Brown headed home a corner kick 11 minutes later and the Impact had the goal they needed.

The Impact spent the last minutes of the game holding on. Toronto forward Jeff Cunningham missed an open net and the game ended 1–1. Toronto had won the first game, but Montreal had won the first major contest between the two.

The following year, Montreal lost its first three games in the Canadian Championship, including 1–0 in Toronto. Going into the last game, Vancouver was on top of the standings. Toronto needed to beat the Impact by a seemingly impossible four goals in Montreal to win the title.

Montreal coach Marc dos Santos used many bench players since the Impact had already been eliminated. That turned out to be a favor to Toronto, who won 6–1. Toronto fans refer to the game as the "Miracle in Montreal."

It would take Montreal four years to get its revenge, which again came in the 2013 Canadian Championship. By then, the

Montreal's Nevio Pizzolitto lifts the trophy after the Impact defeated Toronto FC to clinch the 2008 Canadian Championship.

tournament had become a knockout competition. Toronto and Montreal were drawn to face each other in the first round. Toronto hosted the first match and won 2–0. For Montreal, overcoming two goals would be tough.

But a week later the scene shifted to Saputo Stadium. Nearly 15,000 fans were on hand. The Impact were dominant from the start. Justin Mapp and Daniele Paponi scored midway through the first half to give Montreal a 2–0 lead and tie the series on aggregate. Marco Di Vaio added another just before halftime to put the Impact ahead. Andres Romero, Di Vaio, and Andrew Wenger then all scored in the second half. Wenger's goal came four minutes into stoppage time to make it 6–0.

It was the most lopsided score in the first 50 matches the teams played against each other. Montreal went on to play Vancouver in the finals. After a scoreless draw at home, a 2–2 draw in Vancouver gave Montreal the title on away goals. It was the team's second Canadian Championship crown.

Montreal and Toronto met again a year later in the finals of the 2014 Canadian Championship. After a 1–1 draw in Toronto, the second leg in Montreal looked like it was headed to a 0–0 finish. But as the game crept into stoppage time, Di Vaio dribbled to just outside the arc. Then he launched a

Justin Mapp, *left*, celebrates with Davy Arnaud and Maxim Tissot after scoring a goal against Toronto in the 2013 Canadian Championship.

25-yard bomb that caromed off the crossbar. Felipe Martins settled the rebound and buried it. Montreal again had defeated Toronto.

PLAYOFF RUN

The rivals have had dramatic meetings in the MLS playoffs, too. In 2015 Montreal and Toronto met in the first round. The Impact had qualified for the playoffs in 2013, only their second season in MLS. But this would be Toronto's first playoff appearance after missing out in its first eight tries.

They played at Saputo Stadium, where Patrice Bernier, Ignacio Piatti, and Didier Drogba all scored before halftime. Montreal won 3–0 to dash Toronto's first look at the playoffs.

The Impact thought they had the momentum to continue. Three days later, they faced the Columbus Crew in the first leg of the Eastern Conference finals. Montreal won 2–1 on goals by Bernier and Johan Venegas. But a week later in Ohio, Ethan Finlay scored in the 77th minute to put Columbus ahead 2–1 and tie the series on aggregate goals. The game went into extra time, and Kei Kamara scored in the 111th minute to win it for the Crew.

WHO GOES TO THE CUP?

A year later, the Canadian rivals met again. This time it was in the Eastern Conference finals. The winner would go to the MLS Cup. Montreal had finished with the next-to-last playoff

Montreal's Donny Toia, right, defends against Robbie Findley of Toronto during the Impact's 2015 MLS playoff victory.

berth and was expected to get eliminated early. But it upset DC United in Washington 4–2, setting up a series against the third-best team in the league, the New York Red Bulls.

Toronto FC finally got the best of Montreal in the 2016 MLS Eastern Conference Finals.

Montreal won the first leg at home 1–0 on a second-half goal by Matteo Mancosu. It then had to travel to New York for the second leg. Piatti scored two goals in the second half and Montreal won 2–1 to take the series 3–1 on aggregate.

That set up the clash with Toronto. Before a crowd of more than 61,000 at Olympic Stadium, the Impact jumped out to a

3–0 lead on goals by Dominic Oduro, Mancosu, and Ambroise Oyongo. However, late in the second half, Jozy Altidore and Michael Bradley tallied for Toronto. Montreal won 3–2, but now it had to go to Toronto.

Before an overflow crowd of more than 35,000, the game was a see-saw affair. Oduro gave Montreal the lead in the 24th minute. But 13 minutes later, Armando Cooper tied it for Toronto. Then Altidore put Toronto ahead just before halftime. But Piatti pulled Montreal even early in the second half.

Nick Hagglund put Toronto ahead again 3–2, tying the aggregate score 5–5 midway through the second half. That sent the game into extra time. Toronto finally prevailed. Benoit Cheyrou and Tosaint Ricketts scored two minutes apart to doom Montreal and end its longest playoff run.

That's the closest Montreal has come to reaching the MLS Cup. In fact, the team missed the playoffs in each of the next three seasons. But with new coach Thierry Henry at the helm, Montreal was back in the playoffs in 2020. After that, the team rebranded as CF Montreal. For the die-hard fans who had been around for decades, there was again reason to hope that a return to greatness was just around the corner.

TIMELINE

2004

The Impact defeat the Seattle Sounders 2–0 to win the USL A-League championship.

2008

Stade Saputo, or Saputo Stadium, is opened with a capacity of 13,034. Its capacity is later expanded to 19,619.

2008

The Impact draw 1–1 with Toronto FC to win the inaugural Canadian Championship.

2009

The Impact defeat the Vancouver Whitecaps 3–1 to complete a 6–3 aggregate victory and win the USL First Division crown.

2010

Major League Soccer announces the Montreal Impact as the 19th team in the league.

2012

The Impact play their first game in MLS, a 2–0 loss to the Vancouver Whitecaps.

2014

The Impact defeat archrival Toronto FC 1–0 in the second leg of the Canadian Championship finals to capture its second consecutive Voyageurs Cup and third overall.

2015

A capacity crowd of 61,004 fills Olympic Stadium only to see Montreal lose 4–2 to Mexico's Club America in the second leg final of the Concacaf Champions League.

2015

In his first start with the Impact, Didier Drogba nets a hat trick as Montreal defeats the Chicago Fire 4–3.

2021

Looking to attract more fans, the team changes its identity and takes on the name CF Montreal.

TEAM FACTS

FIRST SEASON

2012

STADIUMS

Saputo Stadium (2012–)
Olympic Stadium (2012–)

VOYAGEURS CUP/CANADIAN CHAMPIONSHIPS

2008, 2013, 2014, 2019

KEY PLAYERS

Patrice Bernier (2012–17)
Evan Bush (2012–20)
Marco Di Vaio (2012–14)
Didier Drogba (2015–16)
Justin Mapp (2012–15)
Ignacio Piatti (2014–19)
Romell Quioto (2020–)

KEY COACHES

Mauro Biello (2015–17)
Thierry Henry (2020–)
Frank Klopas (2014–15)

MLS DEFENDER OF THE YEAR

Laurent Ciman (2015)

MLS BEST XI

Laurent Ciman (2015)
Marco Di Vaio (2013)
Ignacio Piatti (2016, 2018)

GLOSSARY

aggregate
The combined score of both games in a two-game series.

away goals
Goals scored at an opponent's stadium.

cosmopolitan
Including or containing people from many different countries.

Designated Player
An MLS player whose salary counts outside the salary cap, allowing teams to sign stars.

draw
A game that ends in a tie.

folded
Went out of business.

knockout
A kind of competition in which one loss eliminates a team.

leg
One of two matches in a series.

penalty area
The box in front of the goal where a player is granted a penalty kick if he or she is fouled.

penalty kick
A play in which a shooter faces a goalkeeper alone; it is used to decide tie games or as a result of a foul.

stoppage time
Also known as injury time, a number of minutes tacked onto the end of a half for stoppages that occurred during play from injuries, free kicks, and goals.

MORE INFORMATION

BOOKS

Marthaler, Jon. *Ultimate Soccer Road Trip*. Minneapolis, MN: Abdo Publishing, 2019.

McDougall, Chrös. *Toronto FC*. Minneapolis, MN: Abdo Publishing, 2022.

Seidel, Jeff. *Chelsea FC*. Minneapolis, MN: Abdo Publishing, 2018.

ONLINE RESOURCES

Booklinks
NONFICTION NETWORK
FREE! ONLINE NONFICTION RESOURCES

To learn more about CF Montreal, please visit **abdobooklinks.com** or scan this QR code. These links are routinely monitored and updated to provide the most current information available.

INDEX

ABOUT THE AUTHOR

Brian Trusdell has been a sportswriter for over 30 years, including stints with the Associated Press and Bloomberg News. He has reported from six Olympics and four World Cups and has traveled to every continent except Antarctica. He lives in New Jersey with his wife and daughter.